Cameron Rogers

The Wind in the Clearing, and Other Poems

Cameron Rogers

The Wind in the Clearing, and Other Poems

ISBN/EAN: 9783744770996

Printed in Europe, USA, Canada, Australia, Japan

Cover: Foto ©Thomas Meinert / pixelio.de

More available books at **www.hansebooks.com**

❧ THE WIND IN THE CLEARING, AND OTHER POEMS ❧ BY ROBERT CAMERON ROGERS : : :

NEW YORK AND LONDON
G. P. PUTNAM'S SONS
MDCCCXCIV

TO
MY FATHER

CONTENTS

	PAGE
THE WIND IN THE CLEARING	3
THE UNLAUNCHED BOAT	9
THE DANCING FAUN	13
HYLAS	18
BLIND POLYPHEMUS	22
ODYSSEUS AT THE MAST	26
THE DEATH OF ARGUS	31
LIKE TO A SHIP	36
MIDNIGHT UPON THE BEACH	37
THEORY	38
A SLEEPING PRIESTESS OF APHRODITE	40
DESTINY	42
COLUMBINE	44
AT LAST	46
THE COMRADES	47
NOAH PORTER	48
VIRGIL'S TOMB	50
BARSET WOOD	52
THE GRAY HAWK	56

CONTENTS

	PAGE
A' OUTRANCE	57
SANTA LUCIA	61
TO VIOLET	63
THACKERAY'S BIRTHDAY	64
THE OLD SMOKER	67
THE COLONEL'S STORY	69
SONGS AND SONNETS.	
SERENADE IN SEVILLE	77
AVALON	79
SONG	80
MIDSUMMER NOON	81
IN PRAISE OF DUSK	82
TO A HARVEST APPLE-TREE	83
AN OPEN QUESTION	84
IN BONDAGE	87
THE SHADOW ROSE	88
"I WILL LIFT UP MINE EYES UNTO THE HILLS"	89
THE LOST SHIP	90
LOVE LAY ASLEEP	91
THE ROSARY	92
AN OLD ITALIAN GARDEN	93
RIDING SONG	95

THE WIND IN THE CLEARING.

THE WIND IN THE CLEARING.

I.

"Where are the pines," said the wind in the clearing—
 "The pines that I knew from the slip to the tree,
That braved me and laughed in my face though I loved them
 And bore their sweet breath with me far out to sea?"

From the black, charred stumps in the pasture,
 Half hid by the wild berry bushes,
 Came a voice—" Here are we.

" The axe and the men came among us,
 They stretched us side by side
In the dust of the pines, our fathers,
 Who stood unscathed in their pride,
Till, bowed by the weight of the years,

They fell where they stood and died.
We have walled the settler's cabin
With stout trunks rugged and mossed,
His fire has fed in the winter nights
On the tops where the hawk's nest tossed,
Our bodies are dwarfed and crippled,
And homes for the squirrel and bee,
We are passing, and yet we have served,
Here are we."

The wind blew North, the wind blew East,
West blew the wind and South—
It whistled and whirled, with the whirling world,
And blew rain and snow and drouth.

II.

"Where are the brooks," said the wind in the clearing,
" And where is the song that they sang to me,
While brook joined brook till the gathering chorus
Died out at the voice of the sea ;
The brooks I fed with the rain I brought

THE WIND IN THE CLEARING

    From the sad, kind heart of the sea—
The warm, sweet tears of the Ocean—
    For Nature's tears are sweet,
And the tears of men are bitter,
    Though the world lies at their feet."

Out of the sunny pasture—
    From turbid pools, once clear,
From the troubled toss at the millwheel,
    Came answer, "We are here.
They have checked our flow by the mill-ponds,
    They have fouled us, one by one,
With dross from the turbulent millwheel,
    They have left no screen from the sun;
And they wonder we run so shallow—
    One day we shall cease to run.

"The trout are gone from the riffles,
    The heron has left the sedge,
And our voice is not singing but sobbing,
    For the trees that stood by the edge.

But down in the noisy ship-yard
  Where the sea tides ponder and dream,
We watch the great frames growing,
  We see the white ribs gleam;
And we know the wheels we toss and whirl
  Speed the mills that shape each beam,
That trim the planks of the fair, white decks,
  That fashion the keels for the sea—
One day we shall cease our flowing,
  And yet we have served—
      Here are we."

The wind blew North, the wind blew East,
  West blew the wind and South—
It whistled and whirled, with the whirling world,
  And blew rain and snow and drouth.

III.

"Where are the men," said the wind in the clearing,
  "The men who furrowed this path for me
Through the pines I loved though they barred my way;

Strong were they and ruddy and fierce,
And there were children used to play
By the side of the brooks now sunk away;"
And a voice said, "Here are we.
We are old and shaken, our race is run,—
We sit in the sunset and dream of the sun,
And wait for a rest almost begun.—
We stood like the pines, but were stronger still—
We cleared the valley, we cleared the hill,
We fettered the brook and built the mill;
We started the millwheel on its round,—
And our lives ran clear as the brooks we bound.

" Our children ?—Look in the towns for them—
Another age has troubles to stem
As hard, may be, as our own have been.
But tell us, wanderer, have you seen
Our children away in the distant towns?
Are they tall and sturdy, as once we stood,
Do they grace their birth in the conquered wood,
Do their lives run clear as the brooks once ran

And should we bless them or should we ban
 Could we see them now ?—but 't is far, 't is far,
  We have done our service,
   Lo ! Here we are."

The wind blew North, the wind blew East,
 West blew the wind and South—
It whistled and whirled, with the whirling world,
 And blew rain and snow and drouth.

THE UNLAUNCHED BOAT.

T. G. W.

I.

Upon the dry sand where the winter tides
Have flung the largess of the spendthrift deep,
In the half-shelter of the dunes I sit.
The tide ebbs fast, and glimmering in the sun,
The strip of beach that lies debatable
Betwixt high tide and low broadens apace,
While here and there some rock, outcropping, bares
Its rugged knuckles fringed about with kelp.

II.

See where the wheeling Ring-necks hold their course
And note their plaintive treble ;—strange, how strange
The mediums that Memory employs,
When some poor straw the wind may set afloat

Bridges the chasm that the years have worn—
So even now that far and mournful cry,
Like an enchanted pitch-pipe sounds a note
To which the clearest chords of memory ring.

III.

I think of one I lost beside the sea—
The sea that breaks upon the dazzled eyes
Of them who crest the last green slope of youth.
Mute in the half-noon sun, beside our boats,
Waiting the favoring tide, we stood together
Harkening to the murmur of the beach—
Striving to penetrate with vague surmise
Mid-ocean secrets babbled at the shore.

IV.

But when I launched my craft and turned to him
He did not follow. Now a mist has shut
The shore away from me and yet I know
It is not distant, for at times I hear
The sound of breakers,—still my pinnace beats

About the offing,—still I sound in vain
To find a channel to the open sea.
He has not joined me yet—beyond the mist
His unlaunched boat lies warping in the sand.

v.

The years slip by with eager pace,
The pinnace holds the selfsame place,—
   Drifted about with sand behold
The figure-head's calm, carven face.

A young man's face and open-eyed
Upon the waters stretching wide—
   Forever longing for their breast
Yet just beyond the highest tide.

Those untried timbers ne'er shall feel
The rapture of the sea, the reel
   Along the hillocks of the deep
With dipping rail, with glimmering keel—

That shapely prow shall never grate
Across the tide-washed bar, elate

THE UNLAUNCHED BOAT

To sail the boundless outer sea
Whose floods brim through the Western gate—

No harbor in the islands blest
Awaits thee with unruffled breast,
    No anchorage for wearied keels,
No road-stead of accomplished quest.

Dim through the mists of memory
The unlaunched boat I sometimes see,
    The carven figure at the prow,
The sad eyes gazing after me;

Those longing eyes that may not weep,
Those lips that ne'er shall kiss the deep,
    While near, yet ever out of reach,
The tempting waters curl and creep.

THE DANCING FAUN.

I.

When Time unswathed the ashen winding sheet
  That wrapped Pompeii—city of the dead;
  And once again the Southern azure shed
Its light through ruined court and empty street;
  Lo! From the darkness, where no human tread
Had echoed for a score of centuries,
  Appeared a multitude of gracious shapes,
A pageant of the long lost deities;—
  Hermes and Pan, and Bacchus crowned with grapes,
And all the pleasant demi-gods and fauns
Who thronged the woods and kept the fountains pure.

II.

They could not die—no fear of time had they,
  For they were born of Art and must endure

Whilst Art should live. The city stricken lay
  About them, yet they took nor note nor care,
Of unseen evenings or of darkened dawns ;
  In passing years they had no place, no part,
Until at last the soft Italian day
  Peered in upon them standing silent there,
  Divine in the divinity of Art.
  And one there was, a faun, among the throng,
With limbs forever leaping into dance,
With head flung back, as though he heard, perchance,
  The far-off echo of some lost Greek song.

III.

Thou dancer of two thousand years,
  Thou dancer of to-day,
What silent music fills thine ears,
  What Bacchic lay,
That thou shouldst dance the centuries
  Down their forgotten way?

What mystic strain of pagan mirth
  Has charmed eternally

Those lithe strong limbs, that spurn the earth?
  What melody,
Unheard of men, has Father Pan
  Left lingering with thee?

Ah! where is now the wanton throng
  That round thee used to meet?
On dead lips died the drinking song,
  But wild and sweet,
What silent music urged thee on,
  To its unuttered beat,

That when at last Time's weary will
  Brought thee again to sight,
Thou cam'st forth dancing, dancing still,
  Into the light,
Unwearied from the murk and dusk
  Of centuries of night?

Alas for thee!—Alas again,
  The early faith is gone!
The Gods are no more seen of men

All, all are gone—
The shaggy forests no more shield
The Satyr and the Faun.

On Attic slopes the bee still hums,
On many an Elian hill
The wild-grape swells, but never comes
The distant trill
Of reedy flutes, for Pan is dead,
Broken his pipes and still.

And yet within thy listening ears
The pagan measures ring—
Those limbs that have outdanced the years
Yet tireless spring,—
How canst thou dream Pan dead when still
Thou seem'st to hear him sing!

IV.

Thou gracious Art, whose creatures do not die,
We too have heard the far-off magic song,—
We too have caught the spirit of the long

Soft Southern days and sheen of sapphire sky.

And thus we listen, like the dancing faun,

We in our distant New World haunts and hear

Thy music nearer coming, and more near,

And feel the promise of thy brightening dawn.

HYLAS.

I.

Beneath the waters of the Mysian spring,
The sacred spring whose guardians are we,
My sisters and myself sat dreamily.
Through the clear water far above our heads
We saw the floating water-grasses dark
Against the cloudless sky, and shadows stretched
In the long afternoon, across the pool,
From tall reeds dozing by the sedgy marge.
Silent we sat, and watched the sacred fish,
Swift gleams of amber in the sunlit pool,
And with deft fingers, nimbly twining, wove
Fillets of green from lissom water weed.

II.

Mid-afternoon had come—when low and clear
Along the slender channel which the spring

Sends timidly unto the unquiet deep,
We heard strange voices on the distant beach;
And grating of stout keels upon the sand,
And sound of sailors wading through the surf,
And shouts and singing in the Argive tongue.
Then for a season all was still again
Till, while we marvelled, plashing through the sedge
Came eager footsteps, and a shadow fell
Across the pool, and we beheld a face
Stooped to the surface of the spring to drink,
Bright curling hair that swam upon the pool
And framed a face that Artemis had loved,
Blue eyes, and all the features of a god.
And god we deemed him, never having seen
The short-lived mortal children of the gods.

III.

E'en now I know not how it came, but ere
His lips had more than stirred the pool they met
My lips, and all of us together flung
Our arms about him, dragging him below

To the soft couches of the sacred spring.
Quiet at last he lay, and on his brow
We set the wreaths that all day we had spun,
And with caresses strove to waken him,
Though but in vain; so still he lay we drew
In terror back, not knowing what had come,
Yet fearing we had done a grievous wrong.

IV.

Now night drew near, and once again we heard
Strange voices shouting from the distant shore;
Hoarse voices crying "Hylas! Hylas! Haste!"
Then all we heard was "Hylas," till behold,
Bruising our sacred marge with mighty feet,
Two figures in bright armor stood and gazed
With troubled faces in the darkening pool.
Ne'er had we seen twain like them; even he
Who lay so still and white before our feet
Was not so near divine. Their curling hair
From underneath their helms escaped to fall
Upon their breast-plates, whose fierce burnished brass

Flung back a challenge to the sinking sun.
In awe we sat, lest through the dusky deeps
They should behold their missing friend, and call
Swift lightnings from their stern and fearless eyes
Upon the sacred waters that we guard.

v.

But at the last they turned, and cried again
Their lost friend's name.—All night along the beach
And in the marshy meadows rang the cry,
" Hylas ! Hylas ! Why lingerest thou so long ?"—
And still before our feet he lay, his eyes
Unclosed but dim, and his bright curling hair
About his godlike face.

BLIND POLYPHEMUS.

I.

ALL day upon a grassy slope I stretch
My vast uncertain limbs. About me stray
The sheep I used to watch, whom still I turn
My darkened eye upon, and I can hear
The patter of their feet, stray near, stray far.
I hear as others see, and still my voice
Has worship with the sheep, they come at call.
Sometimes I lie so still the new-weaned lambs
Huddle against me when the wind blows cold,
Sometimes they leap upon me in their play.
They fear me not, my sheep have never feared.
My hand was only harsh against my kind,
And those fell creatures whom the gods gave souls
To vex the Mother with their restless lives.
Aye, such as he, the wily Ithacan.

II.

For one long year I saw him, day by day,
Against the scar-seamed curtain of mine eye,—
His quick frank smile, his eyes that read one's mind
Yet never gave me glimmer of his own,—
His lean strong arms and broad, brown, knotted back,
And his gaunt followers all like to him
As little foxes to their keen-eyed sire.
And each day, for a year, I felt my way
Down to the beach, and washed the healing wound,
And laid my head upon the cool wet sand,
And cried to Father Sea to pay my score,
Tenfold redoubled, on the crafty one;
To drive him rudderless on outer seas,
To drift him wide of port, to suck his men
Deep into eddying water-pits—to death;
And then when, day by day, his blurring eyes
Had strained, to heart-break, for a sight of port,
To show him land, and then—to strike him blind.

III.

But peace has come at last. My brothers deem
Because I rage no more, that I am mad;
Because my sight is turned upon myself
And I see dimly where the brute has lain
That made my heart his lair, and find it foul.
I cannot drive my past into the past,
My memory holds, but I shall curse no more.

IV.

And often I forget,—when at my side
The old ram crouches, legs beneath him bent,
And round his wrinkled horns I grip my hands
And pillow soft my face upon his flank.
Sleep comes—the blind may sleep as sweet and deep
As those whose eyes are weary of the day,—
And at my side the ram lies quietly—
He guards me now, for once I guarded him.

V.

And Zeus grants one delight;—when day is gone,
When night blinds all, my sight comes back to me;

And I can see, as last I saw, the day—
The great blue breathing deep—the black-ribbed slag
That Titans flung from Ætna's forge to cool
Amid the breakers, and away, beyond,
The coast of Italy.—Again I see
The hazy hills where graze my brothers' sheep,
The olive trees that bow themselves and peer
Down grassy gullies, and the timid joy
Of almond trees in bloom.
                        When morning comes
The ewes unbidden crowd about my knees,
And with blind hands grown gentler than of old
I milk them one by one ;—then pasturewards
I follow them who one time followed me.

ODYSSEUS AT THE MAST.

I.

AND so they bound me to the moaning mast
With hempen withes full fast, and once again,
Their ears against the outer world close sealed,
My comrades bent to the slow yielding oar,
Chanting together as we sped along
A song whose cadence, faintly heard by them,
Brought back to mind the fateful plain of Troy,
The ranks of ships, beached on a hostile shore,
And heroes round them by the fires at night.
And every singer to the well-known strain
Kept time in singing, each man at his oar—
Their shaggy breasts with many a scar thick-seamed,
Their brown backs straightening to the pulse of song:

II.

When, high above the swinging chorus, high
Above the mouthing of the listless deep,

I heard the sirens' song, and saw the surf
White on their reefs hard by upon our lee,
And saw the sisterhood of those who keep
Keen watch to lure the mariner to wreck,—
The fell, fair sisters, with their tawny hair
Tossed by the wind about their shining necks,
Strewing their bosoms with the gleaming drift,
And lapped about them like a snare of gold.
And when they saw our nearing galley push
Its brazen prow above the combing waves
That girt the shoals, they flung the yellow hair
Back from their faces and cried out to me :
" Turn thou, O warrior, who hither come,
Turn now and rest, for yet the day is young,
Fierce is the noon-day sun, rest here with us
Till evening come ! "—but no response gave I,
And naught my comrades heard of what they said.

III.

Then they began once more to sing. Ah Zeus !
Such singing, with a beckoning of hands,

Was never given me before to hear.

I knew what fatal madness hidden lay

In every note, that through their symphony

An after-tone of death went quivering,

Yet all my thought was, only let me hear!

And as they sang, upcrowding came the past,

Hope's flame grew cold, to sudden ashes fell

The sharp desire of home and fatherland.

And then a lying vision filled mine eyes,

And all the sea about looked calm and still,

While those who sang seemed beckoning to a shore

With sloping beach and meadow sweeps beyond,

And sunny hills low rising back of them,

And oh! the beauty of the lips that sang!

IV.

Then wild desire and frantic folly shot

Through all my frame, and with a sudden cry

I wrenched my bonds, but tightened them the more,

Straining the cords until they cut the flesh,

Striving so fiercely that I shook the mast,

And shouted to my men to cut my bonds.
And two of them sprang up, but steadfastly
And heedless of my cries they tighter drew
The withes about my limbs, then sank again
Upon the galley seats. Again the song
Pulsed rhythmic with the cadence of the oars,
And straight ahead the steersman's eyes were set
As though he saw, slow rising on the line
Where meet the lips of Sky and Father Sea,
The rocky skirted isle that was our home ;
As though he saw at sport along the shore
The babes that we had left in swaddling clothes,
And heard the murmur of the narrow streets
That seam the cliffs of far-off Ithaca.
And I, whose standard they had clung about,
Whose flame of fortune they had fed and fanned,
Would fain have turned them to their utter wreck,
And strewn their bones along the sunken reefs
That prop the seats whereon the sirens sing !

V.

But Pallas stood my friend yet once again,
And ever fainter as we held our course
The singing fell upon my panting soul,
Until all sound was dead except the plash
Of tired oar-blades catching at the sea;
For from sheer weariness my comrades' song
Had ceased, and lying breathless on their oars
They gazed at me with their deep sunken eyes
And read my will, and took my stiffened frame
Down from the mast, and with glad hearts set free
Their captive sense. Then presently again
They fell upon the oars, for we could hear
Low breathed along the sultry wind a sound,
Not of the sirens' song alluring us,
But the wild charging cry of waves that stormed
That fearful pass, flanked by twin caverns, where
Charybdis and her sister Scylla watch.

THE DEATH OF ARGUS.

I.

His mighty arms were bare,—his beggar's garb
Showed through its rents the massy chest beneath
On which his tangled beard fell full, his face
Was lean and browner than the russet rocks,
And from their deep-sunk sockets his dark eyes
Burned through the ashes of a thousand hopes.

II.

Now, it befell that children were at play
Upon the beach this day, with treasures trove
Of ocean shores; quaint, living, star-shaped things,
Tresses of sea-weed like to women's hair,
And glossy tangles of the ribbon grass.
Fain had Odysseus joined them, for his heart
Went out to them, the laughing half-grown lads,

Sons of the half-grown lads who years before
Cheered the swift galleys headed towards the East
To that fierce leaguer round the walls of Troy;
But though his voice was kind, they drew apart
In sudden apprehension, as if he
Were some strange creature of the main, some shape
Wild and sinister from the tameless sea.

III.

He laughed and hoarsely through his laughter ran
Sounds as of surf, half anger and half grief;
The laugh of one who lived upon the sea,
Who knew its bitter mirth and long complaint;
Then up the cliff he clomb and left the shore
And wandered in the outskirts of the town,
Till, coming on an open gate, he paused,
For there, beside a hovel's door, prone stretched
Within the sunlight, Argus lay asleep.

IV.

Prone in a patch of sunlight Argus lies,
Argus the hound, the keen Mollossian dog

Odysseus loved and praised ere yet his ships
Sailed Troyward to the long enduring war
A score of years gone by,—his shrivelled form
Scarce shapes the rugged skin that covers it,
His strong legs now but serve his only heed,
To drag him from the shadow to the sun,—
His shrunk lips cling against his toothless jaws;
Those eyes that ever first beheld the stag
Like some dun shadow darting through the wood,
Are darkened now, and the deep-throated cry
That roused on every cliff the echo-sprites
Is scarce a whine to beg a daily crust.

v.

The old dog dreams, and sudden quivers run
Along his withered flank, and fitfully
His great paws move, for once again he seems
To lead the chase, to pull the quarry down,
To see the huntsmen breathless gathering in;
And over all he hears the clear-toned voice
Of one who calls him "Argus, prince of dogs,"
And buffets playfully his mighty head.

VI.

The hunt still sweeps along the rocky paths
And through the wood with hound and net and spear;
And still from rocky cleft and forest nook
The little echo gods peer forth and gibe;—
But nevermore, with half admiring spleen,
They swell their pigmy chests and vainly strive
To mock the deep, far-sounding, clamorous cry
Of Argus, leading all the clean-limbed hounds.

VII.

Into his dream again the well known voice
Breaks suddenly—he hears his master say
"Argus, do you like all the rest forget?"
He wakes, he knows the unforgotten tones,
He strives to whine, to lift himself, in vain,
His breath comes short, his limbs are powerless:
Yet still his head and ears a little move,
His tail stirs feebly and his sightless eyes
Turn upwards piteously as if to say:
"Oh master mine, lo I remember thee,—

But I am old and weak and near to death—
I cannot fawn and leap and be thy dog,
Thy dog of old—I cannot show the love
That I have kept so long for one caress,—
But, master, I have not forgotten thee."
Then came a sudden gasping, quivering sigh,
And he who loved and knew not to forget,
Argus, the hound Odysseus loved, was dead.

VIII.

Then shed Odysseus the first bitter tears
Since to his own he came to find his own
Forgetful of him. Ofttimes had he wept
In various sorrows and few tears were left
To soften the tense cordage of his heart;
But, on the withered form before his feet,
The poor shrunk image of what once had been
The keen companion of his happier years,
The tears fell swiftly; bitter, burning tears
From that hot, wounded yet unconquered heart.

LIKE TO A SHIP.

Like to a ship, upon a shoreless ocean,
   Manned by an ever-growing crew of years,
My life slips onward and with vain devotion,
   My soul stands silent at the helm and steers.

If one strong wind would blow direct and single,
   Then would I turn wherever it might call,—
But many winds there are, that madly mingle,
   And I must trim my sails to favor all.

So whether I be drifting or be sailing,
   I know not and alas shall never know:
My life is one desire, unavailing,
   That some strong settled single wind would blow.

MIDNIGHT UPON THE BEACH.

No sound of life was heard, the plover long
    Had sought amid the reeds a safe retreat ;
The lark was dreaming of her morning song
    In yonder meadow deep amid the wheat.

A drowsy stillness brooded o'er the deep,
    The very air with dreaminess was fraught ;
The murmur of the ebb tide in its sleep,
    Was all the sound the listening night wind caught.

THEORY.

> "Sunt geminæ Somni portæ . . .
>   Altera candenti perfecta nitens elephanto;
>   Sed falsa ad cœlum mittunt insomnia manes."
>
> <div align="right">Virg. <i>Æn.</i>, lib. vi.</div>

She was so beautiful I could but follow;
  Her words seemed truth itself, I could not doubt,
And so she led me out beyond the hollow
  Half-hearted living of the world about.

Steep though the upward path without misgiving
  I followed as she led, and more and more
She grew to seem the guide to that true living
  That I had set my life to looking for.

Footsore I grew and faint, through never nearing
  The goal, yet hopeful ever of the prize,—

When suddenly athwart my path appearing
   I saw a distant gleaming barrier rise ;—

A sheer white wall, pierced by a single gateway,
   Guarding twin doors of ivory finely cut,
Twin doors that as I neared them opened straightway,
   And passed my leader through and swiftly shut.

But when I came and stood beside them knocking,
   And strove to move the strong-joined silent beams,
Forth came a voice in sadness half, half mocking,
   " Thou fool, go back, this is the gate of dreams."

A SLEEPING PRIESTESS OF APHRODITE.

She dreams of Love upon the temple stair—
   About her feet the lithe green lizards play
In all the drowsy, warm, Sicilian air.

The winds have loosed the fillet from her hair ;
   Sea winds, salt-lipped, that laugh and seem to say :
" She dreams of Love, upon the temple stair,

" Then let us twine soft fingers, here and there,
   Amid the gleaming threads that drift and stray
In all the drowsy, warm, Sicilian air,

" And let us weave of them a subtle snare
   To cast about and bind her, as to-day
She dreams of Love, upon the temple stair."

Alas, the madcap winds, how much they dare!
   They wove the web, and in their wanton way,
In all the drowsy, warm, Sicilian air,

They bound her sleeping, in her own bright hair.
   And as she slept came Love—and passed away—
She dreams of Love, upon the temple stair,
In all the drowsy, warm, Sicilian air.

DESTINY.

To one she gave a rose and said,
  " See to it well it does not die."
To one a bunch of poppies red,
  " Lo, guard them well," then bade good-bye.

The slow years came, the slow years went—
  A stately rose tree upward grew—
To every summer flung its scent,
  With every summer bloomed anew.

The slow years went, the slow years came,
  Thickly before an empty shrine
The poppies stood, like sprays of flame,
  Like sunbeams shot through Chian wine.

He of the rose, his whole career
  Was like the rose, Fate's early dower,—

Success pursued him year by year,
    And year by year came fame and power.

He of the poppies—No one wept
    His end, though last of all his line,
For through his life his soul had slept,
    And dreamed, before an empty shrine.

COLUMBINE.

PERHAPS she had sung it an hundred times,
   That same little song with its waltz-time catch,
And its quiver and trill like the crazy chimes,
   On Harlequin there with his paint and patch.

But somehow to-night in its lightest part,
   Some chord she touched not quite the same,
Some chord that quivered about her heart
   For into her eyes a swift mist came;

And I thought; "just then for a little while
   She thought of the time when life was sweet,
Ere the world seemed masked in a painted smile
   Like the wanton Harlequin there at her feet—

"When living was not all pantomime,
   And she only sang when her heart was gay

As it often was in that dear lost time ";
   And yet perchance the whole thing lay

In a twinging pain from her narrow shoe,
   Or the lights with their glitter and glare and dance,
Or the fear of a hiss when the song was through,
   So much lies after the word—" perchance."

Over at last, the song—Once more
   Pantaloon romps in his maudlin style,—
Again the audience yawn or roar,
   At the wanton clown with his painted smile.

AT LAST.

> " Strew on her roses, roses—
> And never a spray of yew."
> MATTHEW ARNOLD.

THE last few words have been spoken,
   The ashes have rung on the bier,
And some there be almost heart-broken,
   But I have shed never a tear.

She pondered life's problem as I did,
   She pined in its limits and thrall,
And now it has all been decided,
   And now she knows nothing or all.

I shed not a tear—for weeping
   Were folly for one who has gone
To the rest of an endless sleeping,
   Or the light of a long-sought dawn.

THE COMRADES.

A SHAPE came striding down the road,
   His locks were gray and stern his mien,—
   His lean hand gripped a sickle keen,
And all men shunned him as he strode.

But seated on a broken shaft,
   Where once a sculptured god had been,
   Remained a figure gaunt and thin,
Who looked into his face and laughed.

The reaper halted—at his breath
   The waning sunlight, shivering, fled,—
   And slowly to the mocker said:
"Rash loiterer, my name is Death."

The other flung his faded hair
   Into the wind and laughed once more;
   "Thou art my trusty friend of yore,"
He said—"for I am called Despair."

NOAH PORTER.

Obiit March, 1892.

Alike all loved him,—careful student, drone,
   Scapegrace or steady man, all knew
His mild reproof was for their good alone,
   And his reproofs were few.
No man remembers him to have his heart
Tingle with some keen unforgotten smart.

Small gift of comeliness had he, scant grace
   Of bearing, little pride of mien,
He had the rugged old-time Roundhead face,
   Severe and yet serene;
But through his clear unwavering eyes of blue
The soul shone fearless, steadfast, calm, and true.

And when at times he smiled I always thought
    Of early rare New England springs,—
Of sudden fleeting April sunbeams caught
    Amid some farm that clings
Rock-sown, ill paying them who strive to till,
Along the crest of a New England hill.

He loved the truth ; the vision of his mind,
    Discerning, clear, he would not dim
With half true compromise,—he cast behind
    All that rang false to him.
His work is over now, his labor done,
His requiescat well and fully won.

The college elms are sleeping, winter still
    Broods in the sap, but soon their veins
Under the waxing April suns will thrill,
    And soon come April rains
And they will wake and bow themselves and wait
For sight of one for whom they wake too late.

VIRGIL'S TOMB.

"CECINI PASCUA, RURA, DUCES."

On an olive crested steep
   Hanging o'er the dusty road,
   Lieth in his last abode,
Wrapped in everlasting sleep,

He who in the days of yore
   Sang of pastures, sang of farms,
   Sang of heroes and their arms,
Sang of passion, sang of war.

When the lark at dawning tells,
   Herald like, the coming day,
   And along the dusty way
Comes the sound of tinkling bells

Rising to the tomb aloft,
   While some modern Corydon
   Drives his bleating cattle on
From the stable to the croft;

Then the soul of Virgil seems
To awaken from its dreams,
To sing again the melodies
Of which he often tells,—
   The music of the birds,
   The lowing of the herds,
The tinkling of the bells.

BARSET WOOD.

COLONIAL NEW ENGLAND.

The clouds hung close on Bolton hill,
 Through Barset wood the wind was sighing,
And now and then when it was still,
 The distant bay was heard replying.
Half down the hill from Barset wood
The " Plow and Anvil " tavern stood.

" This night ten years—" the landlord said,
 "When coming from the Squire's shearing,—
Old Rover there was on ahead,—
 We found the corpse in Whitewood clearing,
All writhed and bleeding, torn and hacked.
God curse the knave who did the act !

Next day we found a bloody trail,
    Through Barset wood and down the hollow
And to the shore ; 't was no avail,
    And at the shore we ceased to follow,—
For there the tide the scent had drowned ;
And that was all we ever found."

The landlord ceased ; the gossips drew
    Their chairs up closer to the fire,
Each told the little that he knew,
    While out of door the gale rose higher—
When suddenly rang out the beat
Along the road, of horses' feet.

The landlord opened wide the door,
    Out through the night the light went flaring,
And from the darkness, covered o'er
    With spattered mud, a horse came bearing
A man with eyes and hair of jet
Above a pale face strangely set.

"A glass of ale"—he drank and paid—
"God's curse," he said, "how black it's growing!"
The landlord ventured, half afraid,
 To hope he was no farther going;—
"Why not?" he said, "I know the way
Blindfold 'twixt here and Southam Bay."

"Yet stay," all urged; "the night is dark,
 Such heavy clouds the moon are veiling,
The road is steep and rough, and hark!
 The storm in Barset wood is wailing—
The wood is haunted"—so they said,
And through the wood the highway led.

"Stand back!" he said; "an old wife's tale
 That children shudder at and dream on,
What do I care for moaning gale,
 For shrouded ghost or spectre demon!"—
The landlord loosed the horse's head
And off into the dark he sped.

All night the wind in Barset wood
   Moaned like a child of horror dreaming,
And farmers swore by bad and good
   They saw the ghost-lights pale and gleaming
Pass through the hemlocks gaunt and old
And vanish in the haunted wold.

And one who with his dog and gun
   In Barset wood had been belated,
Saw down the swale a gray horse run
   Who seemed with a strange burden freighted.
Two figures rode it as it ran,
And one was not a living man.

And at the cliff above the bay,
   The man who kept the light-house tower
Saw, at what time he could not say,
   Though 't was about the midnight hour,
A breathless horse with riders twain
Dash seaward, in the mist and rain.

THE GRAY HAWK.

The great gray hawk, he lingers late
    Circling over the tangled copse,—
Why does he not rejoin his mate
    In the tufted gloom of the pine-tree tops?

Off to his nest in the ragged pine
    The gray hawk flaps his slow-winged flight,
While the early stars begin to shine
    And soft through the wood comes the breath of night.

Look, look there in the tangled copse!
    Is it a man who lies asleep?
See on his face the thick dark drops,
    And what is it gapes in his head so deep?

The great gray hawk has reached his nest
    In the ragged pine above the steep,
All light is dying from out the West,
    And one still lies in the copse asleep.

A' OUTRANCE.

FRANCE, XVII. CENTURY.

"Heigho! Why the plague did you wake me—
    It's barely an half after four?
My head, too, is—ah! I remember
    That little affair at the shore.
Well, I had forgotten completely;
    I must have been drinking last night—
Rapiers, West Sands, and sunrise—
    But whom, by the way, do I fight?

De Genlis! Ah, now I recall it—
    He started it all, did he not?
I drank to his wife—but, the devil!
    He need n't have gotten so hot.
Just see what a ruffler that man is
    To give me a challenge to fight—

And only for pledging milady
    A half dozen times in a night.

Ah, well, it 's a beautiful morning,
    The sun just beginning to rise,—
A glorious day for one's spirit
    To pilgrimage off to the skies—
God keep mine from any such notion,
    This duel 's *a' outrance*, you see,
I have n't confessed for a month back,
    And have n't had breakfast, *tant pis!*

Well, here we are, first at the West Sands!
    The tide is well out,—and how red
The sunrise is painting the ocean—
    Is that a sea-gull overhead?
And here come De Genlis and Virron—
    Messieurs, we were waiting for you
To complete, with the sea and the sunrise,
    The charming effect of the view.

Are we ready? Indeed, we were waiting
   Your orders, Marigny and I—
On guard then it is, we must hasten;
   The sun is already quite high.—
Where now would you like me to pink you?
   I 've no choice at all, don't you see,
And any spot you may desire
   Will be *convenable* for me.

From this hand-shake I judge I was drinking
   Last night, with the thirst of a fish—
I 've vigor enough though to kill you,
   Mon ami, and that 's all I wish—
Keep cool, keep your temper, I beg you—
   Don't fret yourself—Now by your leave
I 'll finish you off—help, Marigny!
   His sword 's in my heart, I believe.

God! God! What a mortification!
   The Amontillado last night—

Was drinking, you know, and my hand shook,
My head, too, was dizzy and light.
And I the best swordsman in Paris!
No priest, please, for such as I am—
I 'm going—Good-bye, my Marigny;
De Genlis, my love to Madame."

SANTA LUCIA.

In Naples' streets, long years gone by,
  I heard the tune he plays to-day ;—
    I wonder if he sees with me
    The brimming streets, the sun-seamed quay,
The sapphire of the southern sky
  With sheen full flung upon the bay.

His violin is out of tune,
  And yet it summons, clear and true,
    The perfect harmony that broods
    Above those sunny latitudes
Where "it seemed always afternoon"—
  I wonder if he feels it too ?

Alas I fear he only sees
  Cold glances at his outstretched hat ;

The long extent of dreary street

Ill cheered by glints of sun that beat,

Half shivering, through the leafless trees,—

And, ("Grazzi Senor") he sees that.

Well, comrade, may it swell the store

To bear thee over seas again

To those old streets, where, thank thy tune,

My thoughts have roamed this winter noon,

Where we may meet perhaps once more,

A rivederla!—Until then!

TO VIOLET,

WITH A BUNCH OF NAMESAKES.

THERE is a maid—I am afraid
   To give her name to you—
Who makes great pets of violets—
   I wish I were one, too.

Once in her youth, this all is truth,
   She took some up to smell;—
In some strange way the records say,
   Into her eyes they fell—

And there they stayed—they never fade,—
   She looks at me—sometimes,—
And then—Oh then I seize my pen
   And fall to writing rhymes.

But, sad mischance! My consonants
   Desert—four vowels, too;
A, E, O, I, take wings, that's why
   My rhymes are filled with *U*.

THACKERAY'S BIRTHDAY.

A BARMECIDE FEAST IN ITS HONOR.

OPEN his books and bid them forth ;—
    Come Clive, come Ethel, Colonel, "Pen";
Come Henry Esmond, Beatrix,
    Out into our dull world again.

George Warrington, "Pen's" George, I mean,
    (His grandpapa I vote a prig ;)
Come too, and Major, if you 're dressed,
    And Morgan has arranged your wig :

Come Hetty—Harry Warrington—
    And Bernstein ?—Well, no, as for her—
We 've Beatrix already here,
    And Beatrix we much prefer.

Come Becky, Emmy, Dobbin, George;
  Here 's Captain "Cos" must have a place
About the board, and now we 're met,
  Charles Honeyman shall breathe a grace.

And then Fred Bayham, honest Fred,
  With claret jug pushed well his way,
Shall give the toast, that suits all, most,
  Of William Makepeace Thackeray.

. . . . . .

What, are they gone! Some jarring force
  Upon the vision rudely broke,—
My pipe is out, my guests are gone,—
  They 've vanished somewhere in the smoke.

With nimble feet their way they take
  Down shadowy paths of romance dim;
But I, a lonely Barmecide,
  Drink deeply in my heart to him.

. . . .

THE TOAST.

To him who in the fields of life
    Quickly discerned the vulgar chaff,—
And knew it void of honest grain,
    And blew it from him with a laugh.

To him whose laughter none the less
    Was not wild mirth nor wanton jeer,
But oftenest of that rare fine ring
    That finds its echo in a tear.

To him whose pen was never still,
    Who for three decades thought and wrote ;
Who told of life, of love, of death,
    And never struck an untrue note.

THE OLD SMOKER.

When I was young and my hair was thick
    And purse was thin, I used to smoke
Cigars that now would make me sick;
    Yet from their fumes I could evoke
Such visions as I never see
        Now I am old.

Within each rank cheroot rolled tight
    A world of dreams there used to be—
I conquered new worlds every night;
    One such cheroot would conquer me,
        Now I am old.

Some of those dreams I can't forget,—
    And some came true, I've wealth and name;
And one was—but a dream, and yet

I'm smoking still and much the same,
> Now I am old.

I recollect that those cigars
> That brought that faithless dream to me
> Turned bitterest ashes. Let them be,—

Let ashes cover up old scars,
> Now I am old.

I'm fifty odd—my hair is thin—
> My purse is stout, and so am I;

I take not half the old comfort in
> The best *Perfecto* I can buy,—

And visions I no longer see,
And smoke is only smoke to me,
> Now I am old.

THE COLONEL'S STORY.

One night last summer as we strolled
    Under the stars, the Colonel and I,
    He told this story, and here I try
To tell it just as I heard it told.

"Yes," said the Colonel. "I think with you
    That full nine tenths of the fine things done
In the war are barely known to a few,—
    And for example, here is one.

"It is in battle, Antietam, some
    Call it Sharpsburg, down in the corn
Shells are bursting, minie balls hum,
    Saving the reapers trouble, and borne
Along the line from the charging right
Comes the roar of the midday fight.

"Here are two regiments, one in gray,
  The other in blue—so very near,
Barely a score of yards away,—
You fairly see the passions play
  Across the faces and you hear—
  I hear it now, the yell and cheer,
As, firing into each other's faces,
The men load, fire, and drop in their places.

"You can't tell what a battle is—
  Not the least bit what it's like—unless
You've been there and heard the whizz
Of the bullets, and all,—but what's the use!
I can't describe it—Hell broke loose
  Is, mildly enough, descriptive, I guess.

"Fingers that never seem to tire
To load and fire and load and fire,—
Faces grimy with powder and sweat,—
Eyes with the gleam of the bayonet,—
Shouts, howls, curses; the best men swear

In battle—It does n't mean much there.
One thought blazing in old and young,
The wish the minie ball always sung;
And that was frankly, murder, although
In battle we seldom call it so.

"But to my story; I need n't take
The trouble to say that by and by
In such a fire, one side must break;
And suddenly under the drifting smoke
I saw the gray line all but broke
And seemed to be flinching, when a man
Bearing a flag, sprang out of the van
Back to his own and face to the foe
Between the regiments, to and fro,
Flaunting his flag;—a moment or so
And all was over.—
                    Perhaps you think
Men in the heat of battle shrink
   From shooting a man for some gallant act
Some deed like that—Ah well, I know

In fiction they often tell us so,—
    Hardly, I fear, it holds in fact;
Pity 's a virtue that don't inspire
Right in the hell of a hot file-fire;—
'Shoot the damn fool with the flag,' they said:
A hundred minie balls stretched him dead.

"Down he fell all shrouded about
    With the poor torn rag that he served so well;
    We fired again, and then with a yell
Charged, and they broke to the rear in rout.
We wrenched the flag, it is war's hard way,
From the grasp of the dead man, where he lay.

"Dead? Oh yes, but think of the life
    He lived for reward in that little space
When far above the smoke and strife
    His courage flew, and from his place
Waving the flag from its riddled mast,
    He sprang out, facing the shrinking line
And knew the next moment would be his last!—

Why, all he needed to be divine
Was death, and that came on apace!

" Perhaps in some pleasant Southern State
Some there were to wonder and wait,—
To start at the beat of a passing drum
And long for a step that would never come.
Perhaps the only ones who sighed
Were the very men who shot him there;—
Even in war it 's a general rule
The heart gets soft when the head gets cool,
Then, courage is courage everywhere,—
And they loved him for the death he died.

All men are n't heroes, but some men are,"
Said the Colonel, relighting his cold cigar.

SONGS AND SONNETS.

SERENADE IN SEVILLE.

All murmur, all motion is hushed on the Prado,
   Concita,
 No echoing tread in the dark street is heard,
I stand here alone at my heart's El Dorado,
   Carita,
 Waiting for one little word.

Aslant the Giralda the moon pours its riches,
   Concita,
 And through the dark church draws a pathway of light;
The saints are asleep in their shrines and their niches,
   Carita,
 We only are wakeful to-night.

All Seville is sleeping about me, above me,
>Concita,

Alone in the dark I am waiting for hope or despair,
So drop me a token to show that you love me,
>Carita,

Or drop the stiletto that gleams in your hair.

AVALON.

We seek a land beneath the early beams
   Of stars that rise beyond the sunset gate,
   Where all the year the twilight lingers late,
Athwart whose coast the last born sun-ray gleams.
Fair are the fields and full of pleasant streams,
   Far sound the hedgerows with the burgher bees,
   Soft are the winds and taste of Southern seas,
Night brings no longing there, and sleep no dreams.

O tillerman, steer true, while we who bow
   Above the oarshafts sing the land we seek,
     Land of the past, its rapture and its ruth ;
Future we ask none, we are memories now,
   We bear the years whose lips no longer speak,
     And round our galley's prow the name is Youth.

SONG.

Sitting here before thy feet,
Life to me is all complete,
Black-browed Care beats swift retreat
   When we are together, Love !

What care I for changing skies,
I am only weather-wise;
In the heaven of thine eyes—
   Little reck I whether, Love,

Moments pass or hours flee,
What has time to do with thee,
What has time to do with me,
   When we are together, Love !

MIDSUMMER NOON.

From distant pasture lands the bleat of sheep
    Comes lazily upon the wind to me;—
    About my window trolls a vagrant bee
Low drowsy music to the flowers asleep:
Beyond the orchard yellow wheat stands deep,
    And scythes bright-bladed glitter to and fro,—
    And suited to the cadence, rhythmic, low,
Drifts back the measured song of those who reap.

The spider sleeps within his hammock woof,
    The lizard on the sun-bathed dial sprawls;
    Above my head I hear the drowsy croon
Of doves beneath the jutting of the roof;
    While from the zenith with the suntide falls
        The subtle somnolence of summer noon.

IN PRAISE OF DUSK.

For some they love the morning hours,
    The yellow midday some,—
But give to me the twilight when
    The cricket voices come,—

When bright against the hedgerows burn
    The early fire-flies :
For then I meet my sweetheart with
    The dusk light in her eyes.

Behind the Western hill the sun
    Is far upon its way,—
Though twilight lingering seems to be
    An after-thought of day ;

And when we part at dark I know,
    Unworthy though I be,
That in her eyes' sweet twilight lies
    An after-thought of me.

TO A HARVEST APPLE-TREE.

HALF up the trunk a bluebird had its nest
    Hid in the crumbling bole—in peril too,
For oftentimes my clambering feet found rest
    In the same hollow ;—farther up there grew
Straight slender shoots, tributes the old tree threw
    To Nature's law that new must spring from old,
    Then gray forked limbs, green tangles then, till, gold,
High up the apples glittered into view.

Apples that each year fewer came, and those
    That ripened, matchless, water-cored, complete,
    Swung all unseen save by an idle boy.
The old tree grew as oft an old dame grows,
    Crabbed and harsh, yet keeping still some sweet,
    Some gift in secret for a grandchild's joy.

AN OPEN QUESTION.

Menalcas pipes—

              Damoetas sings.

" Phyllis had no heart at all,
  (Soft, Menalcas, pipe in tune !)
But her form was fair and tall
And her voice held one in thrall
  Like a nightingale's in June.
  (Soft, Menalcas, pipe in tune !)

"So, since Phyllis had no heart,
  (Slow now, boy, nor quick, nor gay !)
To supply the missing part,
With her face and woman's art,
  She has stolen mine away.
  (Slow now, boy, nor quick, nor gay !")

        Damoetas pipes—

                        Menalcas sings.

" Phyllis had a heart of old,
   (Pitch a tune for lovers' feet !)
For I watched her life unfold
Like a meadow marigold,
    Sweeter maid one may not meet.
    (Pitch a tune for lovers' feet !)

" All things have a cause you see ;
   (Soft now, gently, if you will !)
When she stole your heart from thee
She had lost her own to me.
    Jealously I guard it, still.
    (Soft now, gently, if you will !")

        Damoetas—
" Pan ! What gross effrontery !
   (Let her choose the one most dear !)
Even Delia laughs at thee !
        Menalcas—

Delia laughs from jealousy ;—
Listen ! Phyllis' voice I hear.
   (Let her choose the one most dear ! ")

   Menalcas and Damoetas—
" Come ! We see you loitering there ;—
   (What is this that may have chanced ?)
Laughing Phyllis, tall and fair—
What ! Young Daphnis with her there ?
Have we piped while others danced ?
   (What is this that may have chanced ? ")

IN BONDAGE.

The bay, a burnished blue, beneath the skies,
   Lies almost captive in the mystic charm
   Of dim black headlands, with one silver arm
Linked with the Mother sea, beyond that lies.
Across the languid lift a sea bird plies
   From shadeless shore, to shadeless shore away,
   And far below, upon the breathless bay,
A shadow bird pursues it, as it flies.

O sleeping bay, my heart asleep with thee,
   Is prisoner in the lands of yesterday;
     Those far fair lands, along whose drowsy streams
The voices, calling from the outside sea,
   Meet no response, and baffled, die away,
     Unheeded on the dim frontier of dreams.

THE SHADOW ROSE.

A NOISETTE on my garden path
   An ever swaying shadow throws;
But if I pluck it strolling by,
   I pluck the shadow with the rose.

Just near enough my heart you stood
   To shadow it,—But was it fair
In him, who plucked and bore you off,
   To leave your shadow lingering there?

"I WILL LIFT UP MINE EYES UNTO THE HILLS."

There is no joy upon the mountain's side;
  Below the meadows lie, and dull content,
  The swift bees following the clover scent,
The peasant, like his oxen, heavy-eyed.
But far above, where whirling cloud-scarves hide
  The sentry crags' gray, flinty armament,
  The spirit straightens like a bow unbent,
Filled with the rapture of dim paths untried.

Sweet is the valley music,—Sweet the hum
  Of bees,—but on beyond the upland mist
    Which sets false barriers to feeble wills,
Are triumph tones, sonorous chords that come,
  As from the touch of some strong organist
    Hidden amid the transepts of the hills.

THE LOST SHIP.

Along the shore of the sunset
    The sombre cloud-drifts lie,
Dark shoals in the yellow ocean
    That floods through the Western sky.

And I often stand in the twilight
    When the West begins to pale,
To watch, away in the distance,
    For the gleam of a vanished sail—

The sail of a ship treasure laden
    With dreams of a time gone by,
That sails for aye in the ocean
    That floods through the Western sky.

LOVE LAY ASLEEP.

Love lay asleep one noon in dim Cathay,
   And as he slept Fate passed, and having seen
   The bow still strung, the sheaf of arrows keen,
From out the quiver stole two shafts away.
Fate with her calm face, neither grave nor gay,
   Fate without heart, who neither weeps nor smiles,
   Launched them, and through ten thousand weary miles
They found a mark within our hearts that day.

Shall we blame Love, because thy lips and mine
   Must smile on all the world, yet never touch?
   Shall we blame love for that keen archery
That stung with sweet despair my heart and thine?
   Ah no, blame Fate, yet blame not over-much,
   For Love is blind, and might have passed us by.

THE ROSARY.

The hours I spent with thee, dear heart,
    Are as a string of pearls to me ;
I count them over, every one apart,
        My rosary.

Each hour a pearl, each pearl a prayer,
    To still a heart in absence wrung ;
I tell each bead unto the end and there
        A cross is hung.

Oh memories that bless—and burn !
    Oh barren gain—and bitter loss !
I kiss each bead and strive at last to learn,
        To kiss the cross,
            Sweetheart,
                To kiss the cross.

AN OLD ITALIAN GARDEN.

I.

The gate is long since gone ; where once it stood,
   Marking the spot, twin carven pillars bide ;
   Within two lichened walls go, side by side ;
A tiled way lies between, all overhung
With branches drowsy ilex trees have flung
   Across the walls : branches half breathless, spread
   Like hands bespeaking silence,—overhead
One locust tests his viol, tensely strung.

Upon the tiles, slow weaving through the loom
   Of leaves, the noon flings dusky tapestries ;
And here is shadow with no hint of gloom,
   And sunlight here is gentle to the eyes.
The garden lies beyond, half-seen, unknown,
Lulled by a hidden fountain's monotone.

II.

The garden sleeps and dreaming deep it sees,
   Green alleys haunted by the gods of eld ;
   Again the slender calamus is held
To lip of faun, and reedy melodies
Call up shy Echo couched amid the trees.
   The gods throng back into the days that be—
   Old dreaming garden, I will dream with thee,
And people sleep with lost divinities.

One god alone will stray into my sleep,
   A tearful boy, out-barring all the rest.
   Ah, bitter lot, that he should be supreme,
And yet with blind eyes too compelled to weep !
   Poor play of shallow words, when truth is best,—
I have not slept, and he is not a dream.

RIDING SONG.

MAKING tide, and a midnight moon;
   Where do we ride to-night?
White to seaward, white each dune,
   White as the surf is white.
Hoofs of horses, steady, in tune,
   Beat like a pulse of the night.

Bit to bit and an easy rein,
   Neither of us to lead;
I will forget the course is vain,
   Time and to spare for heed,
When the moon dips down and the planets wane,
   And a dark dawn checks the speed.

Flood-tide, and now we ride,
   Hark to the eight-hoof beat!

Fetlock deep, when the spent waves hide
    Track of the galloping feet:
Life swings free, the world sweeps wide,
    Breath of the sea blows sweet.

Then ride, for dawn is swift and sure,
    And an ebb must always be;
This magic moon will but endure
    One hour more up from the sea.
The gold of a year of sun's too poor
    To buy that hour of me!

Though it has no thread in the loom of the past,
    Though a future has been denied,
Though I may not hold it, riding fast,
    And it die, die, die, as we ride;
The rim of the moon has touched at last,
    And here is the turn of the tide.

Oh never for me a moon shall rise
    To shine as this moon has shone;

Like a bark aflame, hull-down, it lies,
   Like a spent flame sunk it has gone,
To shine, where a haunted flood-tide cries
   To the coasts of Avalon.

THE END

www.ingramcontent.com/pod-product-compliance
Lightning Source LLC
Chambersburg PA
CBHW031411160426
43196CB00007B/980